Weatherwise

Wind and Storms

Robyn Hardyman

Published in paperback in 2014 by Wayland
Copyright © Wayland 2014

Wayland, 338 Euston Road, London NW1 3BH
Wayland Australia, Level 17/207 Kent Street, Sydney, NSW 2000

British Library Cataloguing in Publication Data
Hardyman, Robyn
Wind and storms. – (Weatherwise)
1. Winds – Juvenile literature 2. Storms – Juvenile literature
I. Title
551.5'5

Produced for Wayland by Calcium
Design: Rob Norridge and Paul Myerscough
Editor: Sarah Eason
Editor for Wayland: Claire Shanahan
Illustrations: Geoff Ward
Photography by Tudor Photography
Picture research: Maria Joannou
Consultant: Harold Pratt

ISBN 978 0 7502 8146 1

Printed in China

1 3 5 7 9 10 8 6 4 2

Corbis: Abir Abdullah/EPA 23, Jim Mahoney/Dallas Morning News 19, Kelly Owen/Zuma 24,
Neil Rabinowitz 9; **FLPA:** Jim Reed 18; **Fotolia:** Jason Branz 1, 16, Tatiana Grozetskaya 14,
KoMa 17, Yuriy Mazur 12, Sébastien Mirabella 7; **Istockphoto:** Byllwill 11; **NASA:** 21;
Photolibrary: Robert Harding Travel/Geoff Renner 4; **Rex Features:** 27, Bournemouth
News 8; **Shutterstock:** Eric Gevaert 20, Shawn Kashou 25, Robert A. Mansker 22,
Lori Martin 26, David McTavish 10, Melody Mulligan 15.

Cover photograph: **Corbis** (Neil Rabinowitz)

Wayland is a division of Hachette Children's Books, an Hachette UK company.
www.hachette.co.uk

Weath...
the st...
the Be...
starts...
totally...
called...
17 on...

When th...
ground,...
warms, t...
rises up,...
in to take...
flowing a...

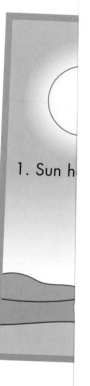

1. Sun h...

Contents

Living with the wind

People everywhere experience the wind. Most people are affected only in small ways – in their choice of clothing or leisure activities, for example. Wind is more important to people who work outdoors. For farmers, the wind might affect their choice of crops to plant and when to **harvest** them. Wind can dry the soil and then blow it away, or it can flatten tall crops.

When it is very windy, it can be difficult to carry out everyday tasks such as shopping.

Unbelievable!

The windiest place on Earth is Port Martin, Antarctica. For 100 days of every year there, winds measure more than 64 kilometres per hour (8 on the Beaufort scale).

Airline pilots and people who work at sea also need to know if strong winds are coming for their safety. People who live in very windy places build houses that can cope with the wind. They are made of strong materials and are built low to the ground.

People who enjoy windsurfing or sailing choose a windy place to go on holiday, for example, Fuerteventura, in the Canary Islands. The word 'Fuerteventura' means 'strong winds'.

Is wind useful?

The wind can be useful to people. On a hot day, a refreshing breeze may cool them down. The wind can be used on water for sailing boats. In some parts of the world, where it is hot for much of the year, **monsoon** winds blow in summer and bring lots of rain. This rain is essential for crops to grow.

People have been using wind power for hundreds of years. Windmills have sails that are pushed by the wind. The sails turn machinery for grinding grain or moving water.

The wind is useful for drying clothes.

Today, wind power is used to make **electricity**. **Wind turbines** act like windmills. Their blades turn in the wind. The energy in the turning blades is made into electricity that can be used in homes and **industry**. Usually, many turbines are built together, creating a wind farm.

? Can remote areas use the wind's energy?

In developing countries, small wind turbines can provide electricity to remote villages and farms. Wind-driven **pumps** can also be used to take water to people's homes.

This wind farm is located on high ground, where the wind is strong and steady.

Thunderstorms

A thunderstorm is a storm of dark clouds and heavy rain. Water droplets build up inside the clouds, which are blown over land by the wind. When the clouds become too heavy with water, they release the droplets, which then fall as rain.

Thunderstorms happen where the Sun is hot and the air is moist. They are most common in parts of the world called the **Tropics**.

The dark clouds of a thunderstorm can make the daytime seem like the night.

Thunderstorms form when the Sun heats the moist air. The water in the air rises and cools, forming enormous clouds called cumulonimbus clouds. Thunder and lightning are often heard and seen with thunderstorms.

Electricity builds up inside the cloud. It is released as a flash of lightning and it zooms down to the ground. Lightning is incredibly hot. It heats the air around it. The air expands with a loud crack. That noise is thunder.

We see the lightning before we hear the thunder because light travels faster than sound. A typical thunderstorm lasts between one and two hours.

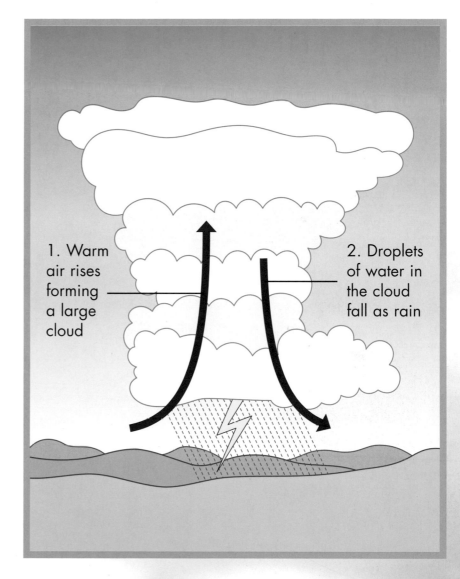

1. Warm air rises forming a large cloud

2. Droplets of water in the cloud fall as rain

Cumulonimbus clouds are formed when warm air rises from the ground and then cools in the sky.

In a thunderstorm

Thunderstorms can cause a lot of damage.
Strong winds can damage trees and buildings.
Heavy rain can cause **floods**, trapping
people in buildings and cars, putting
animals in danger and damaging crops.

The heat in lightning is intense.
It can kill people. Thunderstorms
also sometimes bring balls of
ice, called hailstones. They
can damage property.

*A flash of lightning
lasts for less than half
a second, but it is hot
enough to split a tree
trunk in half.*

Tall buildings are protected from the effects of lightning by lightning conductors. A lightning conductor is a metal rod that is fixed to the top of a building and runs down the side of it, to the ground. The metal takes the electricity away from the building and safely into the ground.

Lightning will strike the rod on top of this building, rather than the building itself.

 **What should people do if they are caught in a thunderstorm?**

People should go indoors if at all possible. If they can't find shelter inside a building, they should lie down – they will be less likely to be hit by lightning. People should always stay away from trees to avoid being hit by lightning during a thunderstorm.

What is a tornado?

A tornado is a spinning funnel of wind. It twirls down from a cloud and rushes across the land, destroying everything in its path. Tornadoes often happen during thunderstorms. They are common in parts of the USA, where they are also known as twisters.

A tornado can travel at great speed, and it is almost impossible to say which direction it will move in.

Tornadoes form when heavy storm clouds suck up warm, moist air. Cool air blows across the top of the cloud. This creates a spinning wind, which twists down to the ground.

Tornadoes often happen in areas where thunderstorms occur. One hit the city of Birmingham, UK, in July 2005. Tornadoes are common in the central part of the USA, known as Tornado Alley.

Tornadoes can also form over water, such as at sea or on a lake. The tornado then creates a **waterspout**.

A waterspout can suck up fish, frogs and other animals and carry them onto land.

? What happens inside a tornado?

Inside a tornado, air swirls around at great speed. A tornado is probably hollow in the centre, but no one has ever been able to get inside one to see!

Harmful tornadoes

Most tornadoes are too small to cause much damage, but some are enormous. Near the centre of a giant tornado, winds spin around at more than 480 kilometres per hour. These are the fastest winds on Earth. Giant tornadoes can travel as fast as a car on a motorway. They cause a lot of damage to land and property.

Tornadoes suck up objects, such as this bike, and then fling them out again at great speed.

People living in areas where there are tornadoes take steps to protect themselves. There are tornado shelters in many schools, offices and public buildings. Some houses also have an underground shelter in the garden. At school, children are taught what to do in a tornado.

Tornadoes damage whatever is in their path. They leave a trail of damage that can be easily seen from above.

 How can people stay safe in a tornado?

People should listen for tornado warnings, then get to a shelter or basement and stay away from windows. If a tornado comes, people should stay down with their hands over their heads. They should not leave the shelter until the all-clear is given. If they are outside, they should lie down.

What is a hurricane?

A hurricane is a huge swirling storm that is many kilometres wide. It builds up far out at sea, as a collection of thunderstorms. It then moves across the ocean and onto land, bringing very strong winds and heavy rain.

Hurricane winds whip up big waves, which can make the sea level rise by several metres.

Hurricanes only happen in a few parts of the world (see map on page 6). They form over very warm seas, mostly in the Tropics. They usually form during the summer and autumn.

From above, a hurricane looks like a huge, white spiralling cloud. In the middle of the hurricane, there is the 'eye'. The hurricane rotates in an anti-clockwise direction around the eye.

Amazingly, it is very calm inside the eye of a hurricane.

Unbelievable!

A typical hurricane is about 480 kilometres across. That is about the distance from London, England, to Edinburgh, Scotland. But hurricanes can be twice this size!

Hurricane damage

When a hurricane reaches land, it brings very heavy rain, as well as winds of up to 300 kilometres per hour. Then a great wall of water called a storm surge hits. Storm surges grow from enormous waves that are formed at sea by hurricane winds.

A hurricane lasts for several hours. There is a period of calm, as the eye of the storm passes over the area. After a while, though, the wind and the rain begin again.

Part of this house in the USA was flattened by Hurricane Katrina in 2005.

Hurricanes cause massive damage. They can injure and kill people. They can cause floods. They can destroy people's homes, and other buildings and property. Cars and boats can be tossed about like toys.

A hurricane can pull trees and other plants out of the ground. The damage caused to telephone lines, roads and airports can make it difficult for rescuers to reach the affected area.

Unbelievable!

In 1991, a hurricane in Bangladesh, South-east Asia, killed more than 130,000 people. It left nine million more people without homes to live in.

This woman rescued a few possessions from the ruins of her house, which was destroyed when Hurricane Sidr hit Bangladesh in 2007.

23

Living with storms

People who live in areas often affected by severe storms do what they can to stay safe. They listen to forecasts on the radio and television, so they know when to expect a storm.

If a severe storm is coming, such as a hurricane or tornado, people follow a disaster plan. This includes covering windows and doors with wooden boards, to make them stronger. They also collect important items, such as fresh water, canned food, torches and blankets.

Meteorologists *use technology to predict where and when a hurricane may hit.*

People in places that may be flooded leave their homes before the storm hits. They listen to advice about the best places to travel to. They only return home when the storm has passed.

? How do meteorologists learn about hurricanes?

Meteorologists fly aeroplanes into the eye of a hurricane out at sea. They collect information about the hurricane that can help predict its path.

In areas where severe storms hit, buildings must be able to cope with strong winds. This skyscraper in Dubai can withstand wind speeds of up to 300 kilometres per hour.

After a storm

Immediately after a storm, rescuers look for people who may have been injured. People may be buried under buildings and trees, or trapped in floods. People whose homes have been badly damaged go to emergency shelters. Here, they are given clean water and food, and a place to sleep.

Water supplies, and electricity and telephone lines, have to be repaired as quickly as possible. It can take months or years for people to clear up all the mess caused by a severe storm. Repairing buildings and roads can cost billions of pounds.

When Hurricane Katrina hit New Orleans in 2005, many victims were made homeless. Some were housed at shelters many kilometres away, such as this Red Cross shelter in Texas, USA.

26

In poor countries, people may be left with nothing at all after a severe storm. In these places, **aid agencies** provide help such as clean water, food and tents.

Why do hurricane victims need water?

Illnesses can spread quickly after hurricanes. This is because the water supply can be contaminated, for example, by seawater and dead animals. Aid workers must get clean water to people as soon as possible.

Helicopters and planes are often used to quickly carry supplies to people after a storm.

27

Measuring wind

Find out which direction the wind blows with this simple experiment to make a windsock.

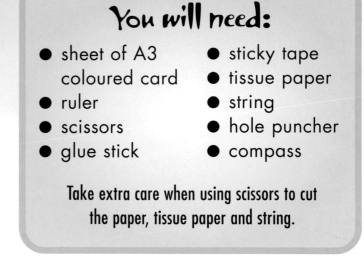

1. Cut the coloured card into a rectangle that is 45 cm long and 15 cm wide.

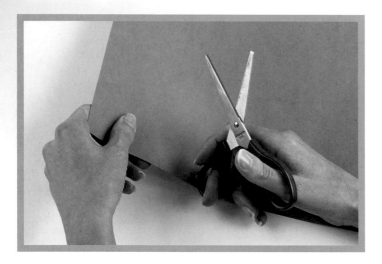

2. Cut the tissue paper into strips that are 60 cm long and 5 cm wide.

3. Put glue along one of the shorter ends of the card rectangle. Stick the strips of tissue paper along the edge.

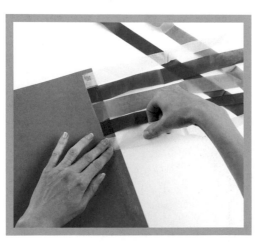

4. Use a hole puncher to make four holes in the opposite end of the card rectangle.

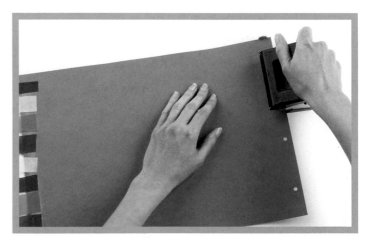

5. Now put a line of glue along one long edge of the card rectangle.

6. Roll the card rectangle into a tube, pressing down onto the long edge you have glued. Use sticky tape to hold the tube together.

7. Cut four pieces of string that are 20 cm long. Thread the string through the holes in your windsock. Tie a knot to hold each piece of string in place.

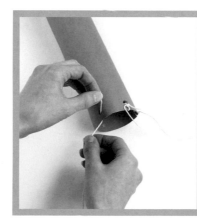

8. Tie all four strings together to make a handle.

9. Hang up your windsock outside on a branch of a tree. Hold the compass near the windsock. In which direction does your windsock move – north, south, east or west? That is the direction in which the wind is blowing.

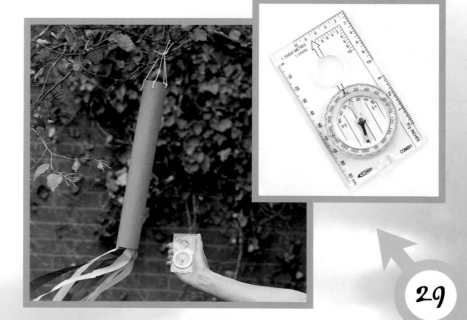

29

Glossary

aid agencies organisations that provide help, such as money or food, to people who need it

electricity form of energy to provide power for light and for items such as computers

floods large amounts of water that cover usually-dry areas

forecasts reports about what weather conditions will be like over the next day or days

forecasters people whose job is to study the weather and work out how it is likely to develop

funnel something that has a wide, round opening at the top, sloping sides and a narrow tube at the bottom

harvest cut and collect crops from the fields

industry activities that make goods for sale

meteorologists people who study and predict the weather

monsoon period of heavy rain in hot countries in Asia

pumps pieces of equipment that cause something, such as water, to move from one place to another

Tropics warm areas of the world, found on either side of the equator

waterspout funnel of water created when a tornado passes over a lake or the sea

wind turbines tall machines with blades that turn in the wind to produce power to make electricity

Find out more

Books

Wind Power (Energy Sources) by Neil Morris (Franklin Watts, 2008)

Wind Energy (Our World) by Rob Bowden (Franklin Watts, 2008)

Wind (Weather Watchers) by Cassie Mayer (Heinemann Library, 2006)

Wind Power – Now and in the Future by Neil Morris (Franklin Watts, 2008)

Websites

Find out more about wind at:
**www.bbc.co.uk/weather/weatherwise/factfiles/basics/
  wind_localwinds.shtml**

Discover more about storms at:
**www.bbc.co.uk/weather/weatherwise/factfiles/extremes/
  storms.shtml**

For more information about hurricanes around the world:
www.metoffice.gov.uk/corporate/pressoffice/hurricanes/

For information, stories and games about tornadoes:
www.nssl.noaa.gov/edu/safety/tornadoguide.html

Index